Poetry
Explorers
2009

North & East London

Edited by Connie Hunt

First published in Great Britain in 2010 by

Young Writers
Remus House
Coltsfoot Drive
Peterborough
PE2 9JX
Telephone: 01733 890066
Website: www.youngwriters.co.uk

All Rights Reserved
Book Design by Spencer Hart
© Copyright Contributors 2009
SB ISBN 978-1-84924-748-1

Foreword

At Young Writers our defining aim is to promote an enjoyment of reading and writing amongst children and young adults. By giving aspiring poets the opportunity to see their work in print, their love of the written word as well as confidence in their own abilities has the chance to blossom.

Our latest competition Poetry Explorers was designed to introduce primary school children to the wonders of creative expression. They were given free reign to write on any theme and in any style, thus encouraging them to use and explore a variety of different poetic forms.

We are proud to present the resulting collection of regional anthologies which are an excellent showcase of young writing talent. With such a diverse range of entries received, the selection process was difficult yet very rewarding. From comical rhymes to poignant verses, there is plenty to entertain and inspire within these pages. We hope you agree that this collection bursting with imagination is one to treasure.

Contents

Gatehouse School, Victoria Park

Emily Hodgson (10)	1
Rachel Crampton (10)	2
Phoebe Gately (11)	3
Adam Shehata	4
Rionach Downing (10)	5
Benedict Sacarello (10)	6
Callum Finn-Reason (10)	7
Daniel Redfern (10)	8
Rachel Moody (10)	9
Maya Nava (9)	10
Felicity Hole-Watts (10)	11
Marcel Kelly (10)	12
Elena Thompson (9)	13
Zakary Cizic (10)	14
Måns Bauer-Molin (10)	15
Larry Boylan (9)	16
Teddy Robinson (9)	17
Eliza Hussain (10)	18
Hannah Cantekin (9)	19
Duncan Rondhout (11)	20
Elias Hirsi (10)	21
Ethan Andrews (9)	22
Kenzie Callander-Cole (9)	23
Joseph Deighton (9)	24
Tobias Hendricks (9)	25
Nadia Hirsi-Petch (9)	26
Olivia Houghton (9)	27
Melike Korbay (9)	28
Lesley-Anne Okafor (9)	29
Ellen Pallant (9)	30
Eleanor Piggot (9)	31
Lorena Pipenco (9)	32
Molly Veitch-Hodges (10)	33

Handsworth Primary School, Highams Park

Olivia Dean (10)	34
Natashka Hayles-Downes (8)	35
Nidaa Mahmood (9)	36

Leopold Primary School, Willesden

Litchina McKenzie (8)	37
Catriona Ison (7)	38
Genie-Jo Matheson (7)	39
Oluwole Orimoloye (7)	40
Shakeira Ramasar (8)	41
Khaliq Raymond-Callender (8)	42
Kaylem Andrews (8)	43
Riya Varsani (8)	44
Jeamar Rose (8)	45
Andre Ellington (8)	46
Leah McMenamin (7)	47
Davia Lee (7)	48
Jannai Ricketts (7)	49
Ishmael Thomas (7)	50
Rashauna Martin (7)	51
Aspen Morgan (7)	52
Kairie Woodstock (7)	53
Kyra Amiree Foster Bah (10)	54
Oluwasesan Russell (10)	55
Monisola Orimoloye (10)	56
Zite Efobi (10)	57
Emilola Johnson (10)	58
Ndea Lawrence	59
Max Meredith	60
Omair Azim (8)	61
Omarri Lawrence (8)	62
Lina Idris Hashim (8)	63
Tyrese Hafizi (8)	64

Nia Deacon (10)	65
Tega Ovire (10)	66
Laquain Beckford (8)	67
Phoebe Adeoye Otukoya (8)	68
Alexis Roberta Mclean (10)	69
Parisha Dabasia (10)	70
Farid Seray-Wurie (10)	71
Paige Wright (10)	72
Aliya Nsemoh (8)	73
Joshua Bellot-Ryan (8)	74
Dylan Mitchell (9)	75
Timi Akinola (8)	76
Masood Ali Khalid (9)	77
Susan Currie (9)	78
Makere Mimi Powell (8)	79
Jade Meredith (9)	80
Makai Payne (8)	81
Sean Guevarra (8)	82
Emile Jesi (9)	83
Ines Santos (9)	84
Jade Gregory (9)	85
Opeyemi Orimoloye (9)	86
Tyriesha Clarke (9)	87
Lydia Jagroo (9)	88
Lucie Lognon (9)	89
Adetomiwa Adenaike (9)	90
Rose Ellington (9)	91
Ella Mae Stodart (9)	92

St Agnes' RC Primary School, Cricklewood

Rachel Carter (8)	93
Vicky Tsouki (9)	94
Stanley Kasombo (8)	95
Stephanie Orleans (8)	96
Catarina Alves (8)	97
Grace Marquez-Gately (8)	98
Sinead Gallagher (9)	99
Tiffany Eulalio (9)	100
Reece John Lyons (10)	101
Wiktoria Bednarek (10)	102
Aaron Boymbo (11)	103

Natalia Kowalczyk (11)	104
Callum Street (10)	105
Chukwuemeka Ogakwu (10)	106
Paulina Seegar (10)	107
Reece Lareo (10)	108
Hannah Sullivan (10)	109
Lance Castro (10)	110
Leilah Jade Bartley (9)	111
Angeline Castro (9)	112
Angelina Sentamu (8)	113
Leon Lyons (8)	114
Andrea Pamo Simples (8)	115
Lee Smith (8)	116
Adrian Paul Lat (8)	117
Jamie Holgate (8)	118
Stanley White (9)	119
Freya Morrison (9)	120
Xavier Fernando (7)	121
David Oduro Kwarteng (7)	122
Hollie Young (8)	123
Jack O'Sullivan (7)	124
Papa Opoku-Adjei (8)	125
Nana Kwadjo Kwao-Amoako (9)	126
Rhys Alves (9)	127
Shaheryar Nadeem (7)	128
Mallaidh Duffy (7)	129
Anthony Badr (7)	130
Ziemowit Jozefowski (7)	131

St James' CE Junior School, Forest Gate

Ayana Moore (11)	132
Mitchel Chappell (11)	133
Sami Sidhom (10)	134
Ameera Kidiya (10)	135
Kyran Weekes (10)	136
Anika Islam (10)	137
Katherine Strasser-Williams (10)	138
Kennedee Chappell (11)	139
Theodore Nelson (10)	140
Nazifa Shahjahan (10)	141
Sean Diasonoma (10)	142
Jawairya Mahboob (7)	143

St Michael's CE Primary School, Camden

Sonia Khanum (10)	144
Sophie Grace Cooper (9)	145
Kabirul Hassan (9)	146
Rumana Begum (9)	147
Kalyss N'tula Leonardo (9)	148
Miyah Susanna Flavius-Lawrence (9)	149
Mohomed Adul Wasim (9)	150
Darmonelle Johnson (9)	151
Mark Omoboriowo (9)	152
Zak Shah (9)	153
Abdo Khadir (10)	154
Hamida Aktar (9)	155
Masuma Chowdhury (9)	156
Munadia Hussain (9)	157
Ismail Uddin (10)	158
Vesa Sponca (9)	159
Fjolla Aliu (10)	160
Isabelle Rolston (10)	161
Mirza Parvez (10)	162
Dary N'tula Leonardo (9)	163

The Poems

The Polar Bear

He stomped off in the icy snow,
Predators around so he stayed down low,
A large seal, he ran in a trice,
His heavy feet almost broke all the ice.

He broke his claws into the seal's pelt,
The warm seal's body made the ice melt,
Suddenly they fell through the snow,
One sharp scrape and the seal lost a toe!

They splashed right into the cold sea,
The seal had escaped, it was filled with glee,
Not too good for the polar bear,
He looked even crosser than Tony Blair!

Emily Hodgson (10)
Gatehouse School, Victoria Park

Springtime

The sun was shining in the sky
The newborn birds were learning to fly
The flowers were growing in the sun
It was so nice for everyone.

The ice on the pond was melting away
The children were coming out to play
The leaves on the trees were turning green
It was a lovely sight to be seen.

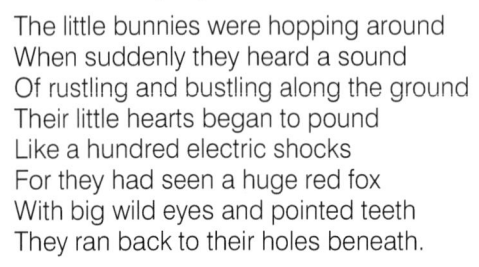

The little bunnies were hopping around
When suddenly they heard a sound
Of rustling and bustling along the ground
Their little hearts began to pound
Like a hundred electric shocks
For they had seen a huge red fox
With big wild eyes and pointed teeth
They ran back to their holes beneath.

The birds chirped out in fear and fright
And flew up to a greater height
The children screamed and ran away
For now they didn't want to play.

Then it was quiet and the fox was gone
The leaves were still green and the sun still shone
Up high in the sky the clouds were gliding
But all the animals were still hiding.

Rachel Crampton (10)
Gatehouse School, Victoria Park

Poetry Explorers 2009 - North & East London

The Cooking Cat

(Inspired by 'Old Possum's Book of Practical Cats' by T S Elliot)

There playing with a ball of string
Being pampered like a royal king
Is a cat who has two white socks
Beside his owner Annie with golden locks

He kills a lot of mice to eat
Knowing they'll be a delicious treat
He enjoys climbing the oak tree
Doing so fills him to the brim with glee

But when the day is nearly done
In the sky there's a moon not a sun
When everybody is asleep
Then outside the house he does stealthily creep

He goes down the deep, dark alleyway
Where he cooks caviar, crème brûlée
Mice stew, tuna and much, much more
All cats that eat some think it's lovely pure galore

When the sun rises in the sky
To all his friends he says goodbye
Through the cat flap into the house
Silently and soundlessly as a feeble mouse

Always looking from the distance
Each day he has a dual existence!

Phoebe Gately (11)
Gatehouse School, Victoria Park

The Old Man

I walk through the streets
watching, listening, smelling
I approach an old man
he has a wrinkly face
he has his own case
he has bloody feet
he only eats meat

He just sits there in the old Amer pub
drinking, smoking
his eyes are blue
he hasn't got a clue
his nose is aquiline

I see him every day
his eyes darting at mine
I watch him beg for money
he's a grumpy old man who needs a home
I usually hear him groaning and moaning.

Adam Shehata
Gatehouse School, Victoria Park

Creepy Haikus

She strolled down the beach
How gracefully she glided
Looking straight ahead.

Her eyes were filled up
Right to the brim with water
She looked so afraid.

She opened the door
The beach house was very dark
So therefore creepy.

A strange man appeared
He turned on a broken light
And said from the dark . . .

'I've been waiting.'

Rionach Downing (10)
Gatehouse School, Victoria Park

The Sky And The Ground

The eagle is a flying killer,
Not an ant it can't see,
Soaring through the sky,
Pulling up any living creature,
The brown for the wisdom,
And the white for the glory.

The wolf is a walking killer,
Hunting in packs or alone,
Catching rabbits and others in a flash,
It is said to be one of the most dangerous desert animals,
It's brown for beauty,
The eyes for danger,
And the thick fur for very sly.

Benedict Sacarello (10)
Gatehouse School, Victoria Park

The Tramp And His Senses

He would stand on the street
Not a finger would move
His eyes would dart around
Watching

His head would move
Every now and again
His ears would be pricked
Listening

His face was as dirty
As a constantly used chimney
His nose would be lifted
Smelling

His face would always
Wear a smile
His back would rub against the wall
Feeling.

Callum Finn-Reason (10)
Gatehouse School, Victoria Park

Science

Pop!
Bang!
Slurp!
Fizz!
A rocket went off with a mighty whizz
The teacher roared, 'What is this mess?'
But to be frank they couldn't care less
A poster on earwigs was ripped from the wall
By a boy named McAndrew McGrubbins, McGrall
While Bert and Ben Baxter were mixing a potion
They were convinced they could make a new hair lotion
Soon Sunny and Henry had got into a fight
About what the speed was of light
Sally giggled and Sunny howled
And the teacher sighed, 'I need a lie down.'

Daniel Redfern (10)
Gatehouse School, Victoria Park

I Don't Want To Learn My Spellings

Please Mrs Dana
I don't want to learn
My spellings.

I have tried writing
Them out but
That never worked.

My head would start
Throbbing
My tummy turned over and over.

You have to break the rules for
Neither, either, eight, veil and vein
So why have rules at all?

The interesting words
I keep in my head
Are replaced by words I can spell.

Please Mrs Dana
I don't want to learn
My spellings.

Can I play
Netball
Instead?

Rachel Moody (10)
Gatehouse School, Victoria Park

Lola Tombola

One Easter Sunday at the fair
With lights so bright and wind in my hair
I pulled on the trigger and closed one eye
As I aimed for the tin and shot it bullseye

The man standing at the counter rubbed hard on his chin
As he reached for the lid of the plastic bin
'Funny looking fish,' my dad said
As the man passed over a bag as big as a bed

I pulled on the strings
And saw
The most
Amazing thing

Inside was a little grey cat
Fit for a king
And there she sat
Eyes the colour of an emerald ring

'She likes worms, shrews and mice,' the man said
Mum says her breath smells like death
But I think she's the best
As I cuddle her on my chest.

Maya Nava (9)
Gatehouse School, Victoria Park

The Forest Poem

Green of the forest
Blue of the lake
Anything this beautiful I could take.

Red of the flower
And the tropical birds
Our planet is like a rainbow swirl.

Yellow of the sun
Shine of the moon
All drawn out in the best cartoon.

Felicity Hole-Watts (10)
Gatehouse School, Victoria Park

Sausage

Sausages are lovely jubbly
I am always in the mood
For a sizzlin' sausage
I have them for my breakfast
I have them for my lunch
I have them for my supper
I have them for my brunch.

When Mum cooks sausages
I always jump and cheer
When I finish my meal
I always ask for seconds
With mashed potatoes and peas
I love my sausages!

I always lick my plate
When my mum goes to clean my plate
She doesn't bother
I love my sausages, do you?

Marcel Kelly (10)
Gatehouse School, Victoria Park

Spring

I watch the daffodils sway to and fro,
My small rubber duck sits by my side,
What's that shining on me?
It's the golden sun.

The sweet smelling sunflowers,
Are resting by my side,
I can smell some tangy lemons,
It's quite a sour scent.

I can hear the little newborn chicks,
Waddling from here to there,
The noisy canaries sing their song,
I listen with care.

Elena Thompson (9)
Gatehouse School, Victoria Park

Running

Running, running, it's so fun
When I run I stick out my tongue
The more you run the more you sweat
And the more thirsty you get.

Everyone is running, why aren't you?
Come on, it's good for your health, have a go or two
Now you're healthy get out there
If you run your best you will be a winner.

Zakary Cizic (10)
Gatehouse School, Victoria Park

Getting Through The Cave

Go 50 steps to the north
and then 20 steps to the east.
Then turn left for 30 steps
now you are at the stairs.

This is the second part.
Turn right and go 70 steps south east.
Then go to the ladder
that you see now, good work.

For part 3 go 100 steps south east.
Then go 10 steps west.
Then take 17 steps east and turn left.
I hope you have got through the cave.

Mâns Bauer-Molin (10)
Gatehouse School, Victoria Park

The Ocean

The ocean is a calm place
It is full of fishes, sharks, piranhas
It is pleasant in every way
It is beautiful
It is a wonderful place
The seas are like emeralds that have grown
You could look at it for hours
The ocean is a sight you will keep in your head forever
So once again I won't deny
The sea is a great place no matter what they say.

Larry Boylan (9)
Gatehouse School, Victoria Park

Crime

Crime is bad
Crime is mad
People who do crime
They're just sad
Don't do crime
Because it's not right
You'll end up in a big fight
If you see someone
Robbing a bank
Don't be scared
But be prepared
To stop them!

Teddy Robinson (9)
Gatehouse School, Victoria Park

Hallowe'en

Hallowe'en, scary, frightening
Vampires, goblins and goo
And everyone at the corner
Waiting to say . . . 'Boo!'

Full moon has risen, shining and shimmering
Owls tooting and cooing
Bats are pitch-black
Jack-o-lanterns, their scary faces are staring
But no one else is caring.

So remember remember the 31st of October
This year everyone will be scarier.
Ha! Ha! Ha!

Eliza Hussain (10)
Gatehouse School, Victoria Park

My Bed

Every night I go to bed
On the pillow you'll find my head
My bed is really soft and cosy
I lie on it when I am dozy.
You and I need some sleep
Let's all hope it's really deep
My mum reads me a story
Whenever she finishes I say, 'Morey!'
When the lights turn off
I sometimes have a cough
My pyjamas are the best
Especially better than the rest
When I hit my bed
No more is said.

Hannah Cantekin (9)
Gatehouse School, Victoria Park

Questions

How does it feel to be older?
Does it make you grander?
Time ticks by like a bird in the sky,
Will time ever stop or not?
Today is Tuesday, tomorrow is Wednesday,
Will it always be that way?

A birthday is your day,
'You're a year older,' they always say,
Every year will I get more privileges?
Or just get hooked up in marriages?
What causes diabetes?
Will the world ever be at peace?

Can I sleep safely in my bed?
What happens when I'm dead?
Should I fear a man with a scar?
Will my work always be below par?
Will I ever stop asking questions?
No!

Duncan Rondhout (11)
Gatehouse School, Victoria Park

Summertime

Summer is like bluebells reborn
Like my life made again.
Summer is fast.
For summer is the best thing I have ever seen.
I love summer.
I feel free!

Summer is like a bowling alley.
And when I go to see a glance.
It has already had its last.
For now it is autumn.
I can hear the raindrops dropping.

Elias Hirsi (10)
Gatehouse School, Victoria Park

The Wacky World Of Footballers

Drogba trips over his own shoes
He wins penalties to make the other team lose.
Ashley Cole shouts at the referee
He doesn't deserve to be on TV.
Tevez left the boys in red
What was going on in his little head?
Rooney scores a lot of goals
In-between those huge white poles.
Messi can run the whole pitch
That's what made him super rich.
Gerrard has a super shot
That's what made all the girls think he's super hot.

Ethan Andrews (9)
Gatehouse School, Victoria Park

The Hockey Game

I play hockey, I'm not cocky
But I'm fast on the ice
I can twist and twirl
And stop on the spot
And score a goal on the ice
The game is quick
As I race with my stick
Forwards with the puck
Wish me good luck.

Kenzie Callander-Cole (9)
Gatehouse School, Victoria Park

The Game

I like playing my game,
It damages my brain,
It makes me go insane.

My mum and dad are to blame,
For buying me this game,
I like to drive a plane,
Or a train,
While playing my game.

When I play my war game,
I always get slain,
I always lose my aim.

I love my games.

Joseph Deighton (9)
Gatehouse School, Victoria Park

Sports

Running in my lane
Pass another runner

Breathing as I swim
Swimming as fast as a fish with its fin

Racing round the track
Tyres getting hot from the friction of the tarmac

As I hit the ball harder
It's 15-love to me and my partner

I kicked the ball into the goal
2nd try I kicked it into the pole

I bet my friends I could score a goal
Through the net I threw the ball

Sport can be very much fun
But when you hurt yourself it can leave you shouting, 'Mum!'

Tobias Hendricks (9)
Gatehouse School, Victoria Park

Autumn Time

Autumn is Nature's time
it feels like a frosty bit inside me.
All around me I see the rainbow leaves,
it reminds me of the spooks of Hallowe'en.

Autumn is time for play
it feels like the happiest time.
All around me I see the shiny brown conkers,
it reminds me of the other seasons but they are not autumn.

Nadia Hirsi-Petch (9)
Gatehouse School, Victoria Park

All Year Bears

January all bears care
February they all go to the fair
March all bears walk under an arch
April bears sit on chairs
May bears rip and tear
June bears eat lots of prunes
July bears like to look at the moon
August bears get married
September bears like to get carried
October bears race up and down the stairs
November bears run like hares
December bears live . . . anywhere.

Olivia Houghton (9)
Gatehouse School, Victoria Park

I Was Sick

On Saturday I was really sick, I slipped over and broke my arm
Like a stick
My mum picked me up and dipped me in the bath
I didn't know whether to cry or laugh
I went to the hospital's A and E
The doctor called to see me
I had an x-ray
They told me to be calm
Then the doctor said I broke my arm.

Melike Korbay (9)
Gatehouse School, Victoria Park

Autumn

Autumn is the time to find a beach hut
It feels like you're a squirrel
All around me I see big fat conkers all around the big wood
It reminds me that most of the animals are hibernating

Autumn is the time to see ghosts and ghouls
It feels like you're a scary monster
All around me I see big ghosts and vampires
It reminds me of Hallowe'en

Autumn is the time to feel chilly and cold
It feels like the right time to worry about winter clothes
All around me my scarf keeps blowing in my face
It reminds me of all the colours of the beautiful leaves.

Lesley-Anne Okafor (9)
Gatehouse School, Victoria Park

Insects - Haikus

Insects are quite small
Ladybirds have lots of spots
They can fly up high

Grasshoppers are green
They jump around the garden
And make strange noises

Beetles can be black
They can also be yellow
And they *click click click*

Dung beetles love dung
Rolling it into big balls
They are so smelly

Butterflies can fly
Butterflies are colourful
They are delicate

Spiders have eight legs
They can run very quickly
And can run up walls.

Ellen Pallant (9)
Gatehouse School, Victoria Park

Autumn

Autumn is a time when leaves fall
It feels like a new world has been born
All around me I see big blankets of leaves
It reminds me of hedgehogs hibernating

Autumn is a time when frost sets on the ground
It feels icy cold
All around me I see tufts of white
It reminds me of wrapping up warm

Autumn is a time when pumpkins sprout
It feels like lunchtime
All around me I see seeds falling
It reminds me of squirrels

Autumn is a time when ghosts play
It feels quite scary
All around me I see pumpkins smiling
It reminds me of spooky Hallowe'en.

Eleanor Piggot (9)
Gatehouse School, Victoria Park

Autumn

Autumn is when all the colourful leaves fall
It feels like the world has changed
All around me I see the ground full of leaves
It reminds me that the trees will be bare.

Autumn is when you see conkers everywhere
It feels like Hallowe'en is coming near
All around me I see scarecrows
It reminds me of all the nice leaves

Autumn is the smile on your face
It feels like I am in a different place
All around me I see the frost coming
It reminds me of Hallowe'en

Autumn is the shiver which is happening
It feels like it is winter
All around me I see my breath
It reminds me of Christmas

Autumn is everything you want
It feels like my hands are getting colder
All around me I see the decorations
It reminds me of the Hallowe'en part.

Lorena Pipenco (9)
Gatehouse School, Victoria Park

Animal Family

My mum is like a puppy
because she is sweet and lovable.

My dad is like a gorilla
because he is funny and a bit loud.

My brother is like a dog
because he is always after a ball.

My grandad is like a cow
because he is weird and greedy.

My nanny is like a panda bear
because she is cute and cuddly.

But I am like Sparky (my dog)
because I am cheeky and always hungry.

Molly Veitch-Hodges (10)
Gatehouse School, Victoria Park

The Dark

I hear a small whimper
And a quick scurry too,
A small feline-like figure
Runs up to you.

There is a small shudder
As the thing hears a bark,
And it gallops away
Into the dark.

I look up at the sky
And stare at the moon,
A great, big, cheesy baboon.

Olivia Dean (10)
Handsworth Primary School, Highams Park

Sally

Sally went to school,
Sally was so cool,
Sally had a beautiful hat,
But her best friend, Molly, had a big cat,

Sally was so sad at that,
She thought she needed her happiness back,
One Tuesday Sally wasn't at school,
She thought she was a fool.

Natashka Hayles-Downes (8)
Handsworth Primary School, Highams Park

A Birthday Wish

Oh my gosh, oh my gosh!
How could it be true?
I've heard it's your birthday
So happy birthday to you.

I think you deserve
To have a big celebration
As when you laugh and joke
It brings a warm sensation.

You are the sweetest person I know
May God protect you and help you to grow
May He always be beside you wherever you go.

Nidaa Mahmood (9)
Handsworth Primary School, Highams Park

My Best Poem

Slipping pasta in my mouth
Marvellous orange making me laugh
Sweet soup slurping on my mouth
Sausages jumping in the pan
Onion makes my eyes burn
Cold fish in my tum
Egg sizzling in the pan
Big fat lemon on my lip
Lovely potatoes jumping in my mouth
Apple crunching in my mouth
Brilliant food in my feet
Sweet strawberries smelling super sweet
Hot hot dog flying in the air
Lovely banana in my hands.

Litchina McKenzie (8)
Leopold Primary School, Willesden

Delicious Diet

Perfect pasta passing down the table
Chunky chicken choking down my neck
Roasting rice racing to my mouth
Tasty tomatoes teasing in my mouth
Fresh fish feeling good down my throat
Racing raspberries tingling my taste buds
Crunchy carrot crunching down my neck
Nutritious nuts going in circles in my mouth.

Catriona Ison (7)
Leopold Primary School, Willesden

My Sweet Lovely Poem

Fantastic kiwi in my stomach
Mysterious milk on my taste buds
Brilliant bananas in their skin
Sizzling sausages in the pan
Chunky chicken in the freezer.

Genie-Jo Matheson (7)
Leopold Primary School, Willesden

My Food Poem

Magnificent melon tasty in my mouth
Brilliant broccoli going up and down
Sweet strawberries red on my lips
Amazing apple juicy in my mouth
Salty steaks salty in my mouth
Tremendous turnips bigger than my mouth
Amazing apricots colourful as orange
King kiwi sweet as a sweetie
Strong seaweed taking out all of my teeth
Marvellous mangoes really nice in my mouth
I'm really full.

Oluwole Orimoloye (7)
Leopold Primary School, Willesden

My Sweet, Sweet, Sweet, Sweet, Sweet Poem!

Sweet strawberries in my mouth
Magnificent melon tasty in my mouth
Delicious salad in my mouth
Delicious potato in my hand
Delicious eggs in the pan
Delicious orange in my body
Brilliant apples in my hand
Brilliant grapes on the plate
Brilliant bananas in the bin
Magnificent pineapple in my body
Magnificent cherry in my mouth
Magnificent pears in my body
Brilliant lemon in my mouth
Magnificent blueberries in my mouth
Magnificent peach in my mouth
Magnificent tangerine in my body
Brilliant raspberry in my mouth
Delicious grapefruit in my body
Delicious lime in my mouth
Magnificent kiwi in my mouth
Magnificent pomegranate in my mouth
Magnificent avocado in my body
Delicious plum in my mouth.

Shakeira Ramasar (8)
Leopold Primary School, Willesden

Wind

Wind, wind you are always here and there
howling through the raging town.
You are like an owl howling through the town and the streets.
Wandering and whistling in the night.
Shaking the tree angrily when the wind passes by.
Wind, you are always blowing sand in people's eyes
at the sandy beach.
Rocking round happily through the town.

Khaliq Raymond-Callender (8)
Leopold Primary School, Willesden

Feeling Poem

Happiness is as red as a rose
Love is like a yellow shooting star
Silence is like a quiet mouse
Sadness is like a sad person.

Kaylem Andrews (8)
Leopold Primary School, Willesden

Silence

Silence is gold and tastes like peace
Silence is red and smells like chips
Silence is yellow and sounds like quiet
Silence is silver and feels like anger
Silence is pink and looks like petals
Silence is green and makes me feel happy.

Riya Varsani (8)
Leopold Primary School, Willesden

Fancy Food

Magnificent mangoes moaning in my belly
Pepperoni pizza piled on my plate
Amazing apples tasting so delicious
Scrummy strawberries slipping down my tongue
Crunchy carrots rolling down my throat
Chunky chicken tumbling down my body
Big bananas bouncing down my belly.

Jeamar Rose (8)
Leopold Primary School, Willesden

Funky Food

Crispy chips crunching in my mouth
Munching mangoes moving through my body
Big bananas biting me in my throat
Slimy salad setting down in my mouth
Sizzling sausage sizzling on my plate.

Andre Ellington (8)
Leopold Primary School, Willesden

Healthy Food

Magnificent mangoes moving when I rumble
Perfect popcorn popping in the pan
Crispy carrots crunching in my mouth
Bonkers bananas bouncing down my throat
Super salad sliding on my plate
Tasty tangerines teasing my taste buds.

Leah McMenamin (7)
Leopold Primary School, Willesden

My Food Poem

Munching mango melting on my tongue.
Crunching chicken cooking in the kitchen.
Big bananas bouncing in my tummy.
Orange oranges obstructing my nose.
Giant grapefruit gulping down my throat.
Sweet strawberries safe to eat.
Chewy cherries churning in my stomach.
Crispy carrots crunching in my mouth.

Davia Lee (7)
Leopold Primary School, Willesden

Yummy Food

Come on everybody have you ever seen a more
mouth-watering sight
Than a pizza dressed up to go out at night?
Thick tomato sauce, mozzarella, cheese,
Sausages, peppers, red and green please!
Sweetcorn, onions, olives, choice pepperoni,
Top it off with lots of cheese.
Hey, add a little spice to make it tastier!
It's looking so good now.
Yummy! My mouth is watering! Hey!
Who took that big slice?

Jannai Ricketts (7)
Leopold Primary School, Willesden

Yummy Food

Amazing apples
Sweet salad
Poking pasta
Punching pickles
Crunching crisps
Big bananas
Crispy carrots.

Ishmael Thomas (7)
Leopold Primary School, Willesden

Favourite Food

Arty apple
Smart salad
Crispy chicken
Perfect pizza
Big bananas
Good grapes
Sweet strawberries
Lovely lemon.

Rashauna Martin (7)
Leopold Primary School, Willesden

My Food

Sour strawberry
Chewy chips
Big banana
Aggressive apple
Perfect pizza
Tasty tangerines
Ping pong peas
Crispy chicken.

Aspen Morgan (7)
Leopold Primary School, Willesden

Fantastic Food

Slimy salad sliding down my throat
Crunchy chips crunching and chewing
Alert apples, I'm alert to the apple
Buzzing bananas buzzing in my tummy.

Kairie Woodstock (7)
Leopold Primary School, Willesden

Beggars Can't Be Choosers

Once there stood a naughty girl
As bossy as a queen
She was owned by a posh family
And was a sprout more than a Krispy Kreme?

Her mother loved her dearly
But her nice behaviour was no more
If there was money
It was off to the store.

She offered to take her
To the mall
'No Mummy no
I want to go to the designer store.'

Beggars can't be choosers
Where have I heard that before?
That's as silly as a clown
As the green monster roared.

Kyra Amiree Foster Bah (10)
Leopold Primary School, Willesden

The Falling Leaf

It was the end of summer
Shortly it would change to autumn
I felt the September sun's hot rays on my skin
All I heard were birds singing
And the crisp sound of other leaves crying
And all I saw were brown, orange, green and gold leaves
I smelt the dying branches upon me
As I fell silently tasting the dust of the Earth
I know that I will be reborn silently in the spring.

Oluwasesan Russell (10)
Leopold Primary School, Willesden

Fruits

Crunch, munch,
Hard or soft,
Pick it, grow it, or get it from the shop.
Wherever you go,
Organic or fresh,
Just remember,
Fruits are the best.
Strawberries are as red as a tomato,
Oranges are orange and get your vitamin C.
Encouraging people to eat fruits,
Before they become sick,
Then at school, you'll get a big tick,
As you can see
Fruits are very healthy,
They make you very wealthy,
Fruits, fruits,
Eat all your healthy fruits.

Monisola Orimoloye (10)
Leopold Primary School, Willesden

Air

Air is here and air is there
To be honest, air is everywhere.

Air is clear but very important
We need air to live
We need air to breathe
We need air to cook and more
Yes, I say air is important,
But also a bore.

Normally, you cannot feel air
You cannot hear air
You cannot smell air
Nor can you see air
But in certain conditions you can.

You can feel air, if there is a breeze
You can smell air, if it is polluted
You can hear air if it whistles by
But it would be a little harder to see air because it is transparent
If you ask me, we cannot live without air
But no one thinks about it
They just carry on with their average day's job.

Zite Efobi (10)
Leopold Primary School, Willesden

Ice Cream

Oh, how I love an ice cream
That light, creamy dessert
Any type of flavour
Another one won't hurt.

Vanilla, butterscotch
Or even a sorbet
They just all taste *delicious!*
In every kind of way.

When I think of ice cream
The colour white comes to mind
It's the lightness of it
Like round clouds in the sky.

Even when I've had three
I know that I've had enough
But the food voice shouts, 'Eat me!'
So to resist is very tough!

I've really had enough now!
I just have to stop
My tummy's very full
I think I'll even pop!

But then the next day comes
I see the cream and ice
Out my hand goes to have a lick
Oh, this is so nice!

Then I stop for a second
My head starts to hurt
I think I'm having brain freeze
I don't feel so alert.

Mum offers me an ice cream
At a party late at night
But I reply, 'No Mum!
I've had enough for life!'

Emilola Johnson (10)
Leopold Primary School, Willesden

Fruits And Vegetables

Cherries and bananas can fill my tummy.
Apples and kiwis are so, so yummy.
Broccoli and peas are the vegetables that I don't eat.
Chocolates and sweets are too bad for me.
But in the end I still like them.

Now my poem is nearly done,
Brush your teeth every day and you will have
Shiny teeth like your mum.

Ndea Lawrence
Leopold Primary School, Willesden

Snow

S now is white, as white as a dress.
N o it is not summer.
O K Mum, no snowball fights.
W ow it is cold, I think I am going to go in.

S now is fun,
N o colds and no illness.
O h yes snowball fights, don't tell Mum.
W ow, good shot.

Max Meredith
Leopold Primary School, Willesden

Love

Love is like sliding down a rainbow
Love is like colouring a heart in red
Love is like getting what I want
Love is like a dream come true
Love is like getting married
Love is like red lipstick
Love is like a bunch of red roses.

Omair Azim (8)
Leopold Primary School, Willesden

Fun

Fun is like a merry-go-round.
Fun is like children playing.
Fun is like the wind coming past.
Fun is like your heart pounding.
Fun is like sweets going through you.
Fun is like a race car going past.
Fun is like cutting a cake.

Omarri Lawrence (8)
Leopold Primary School, Willesden

Love

Love is the friendship ring you have when you are married,
Love is like my dream is coming true,
Love is like the time when I get what I want.

Love is red on my lips,
Love is like birds singing,
Love is like a big heart is in my eyes.

Love is rainbows everywhere,
Love is happiness,
Love is what everyone hopes to have in their life.

Love, love, love, love is what we want.

Lina Idris Hashim (8)
Leopold Primary School, Willesden

Fun

Fun is noisy, fun is cool
Fun is the world's greatest creation
Fun is the colour of cool
Fun is funky like a dancing man
Fun is like being a rock star
Fun is like being messy
Fun is being like a monster
Fun is like Ben 10.

Tyrese Hafizi (8)
Leopold Primary School, Willesden

The Wisdom Poem

Wisdom means you're wise
Obviously there's no surprise
But it also means you're kind
If you share your wisdom-filled mind!

Wisdom often inspires others
Like brothers, sisters, friends and mothers
It inspires them to try and try
Because before you know your time goes by!

Wisdom doesn't just come from old men
Who sit around all day watching children
It can come from children you know
If we practise, our wisdom will grow!

You can see if someone is wise
If you look into their eyes
To get wisdom out of them
You'll have to compromise!

Nia Deacon (10)
Leopold Primary School, Willesden

Dan And Ann Can Do Rap

Dan
Dan can rap all day
He can rap all night
He can wrap up parcels
And tie the knots tight.

Dan can rap in the Houses of Parliament
He can rap while he's packing bins
He can rap in the classroom
And he can rap when he's eating tins.

Dan can rap in Disneyland
He can rap in a bird's nest
He can rap in a chocolate factory
He can rap while he's charging his DS!

Ann
Ann can sing for her supper
She can sing for her tea
She can hum a tune
And swim in the sea.

Ann can sing in the playground
She can sing for a fan
She can sing in a bus
And can sing for Roald Dahl.

Ann can sing for tomorrow
She can sing at dogs
She can sing in Asda
She can hum like a bug.

Tega Ovire (10)
Leopold Primary School, Willesden

Sadness

Sadness' colour is like a blueberry.
It's more entertaining like a movie.
Sadness is the blue colour of two on two.
Sadness, sadness doesn't feel good.
I try not to cry, it feels good.

Laquain Beckford (8)
Leopold Primary School, Willesden

Silence

Silence is as silent as a baby sleeping
Silence is as wonderful as stars twinkling
Silence is like the song, Silent Night
Silence is as deaf as a deaf chicken.

Silence is shocking like a silent statue
Silence is as scary as a skeleton
Silence is as silent as the most silent person in the world
Silence is as quiet as a graveyard.

Silence is like a silent town
Silence brings peace
Silence is like a silent class
Silence is like a silent cupboard.

Phoebe Adeoye Otukoya (8)
Leopold Primary School, Willesden

Wisdom Poem

Wisdom is when you're awake
Wisdom is like a palmy lake.

Wisdom is when you're aware
Wisdom is like a fluffy brown bear.

Wisdom is when you have to make decisions
That can be good or bad
But there are always going to be consequences
That are sad.

Wisdom is when you can be wise
Wisdom is when people don't tell lies.

Wisdom is like a life saver
It changes everyone's behaviour.

Alexis Roberta Mclean (10)
Leopold Primary School, Willesden

When I Was . . .

When I was 1 I sucked my thumb and fell on my bum,
When I was 2 I went to the loo and licked my shoe,
When I was 3 I climbed up a tree and then said, 'Hi Lee,'
When I was 4 I ate some straw and shouted, 'That's raw,'
When I was 5 I was still alive and ate a crab that was so not alive,
When I was 6 I got in a fix and hit my friend Lix,
When I was 7 I learnt about Heaven and met a boy called Steven,
When I was 8 I woke up late and went to bed late,
When I was 9 I jumped in line and broke my spine,
When I was 10 I left my den and went to Big Ben.

Parisha Dabasia (10)
Leopold Primary School, Willesden

Happiness

Happiness, happiness makes me feel
like I'm in a banana peel.
Happiness is the best
is better than all the rest.

Happiness, happiness makes me smile
even after I run a mile.
Happiness, happiness never ends.
Happiness is even in a pen.

Farid Seray-Wurie (10)
Leopold Primary School, Willesden

Ann Can Do Rap

Ann can sing for her supper
She can sing for her tea
She can hum a tune
And swim in the sea.

Ann can sing for her school
She can sing for the loo
She can sing for her pet
And she can sing for her poo.

Ann can rap for her dog
She can rap for her rabbit
She's trying to stop
But it's just a habit.

Ann can dance for the King
She can dance for the Queen
She can do it now that she's 10
And she'll do it when she's 15.

Paige Wright (10)
Leopold Primary School, Willesden

Feelings

Love is as red as a rose, it feels like if you were a star you would
                                        shine as bright as the burning sun.
Joy feels as light as a petal from the most beautiful rose bush
                                              that you'd ever seen.
Silence sounds like the smallest crumb crying out.
Fun looks like children playing on the beach.
Happiness feels as smooth as a baby's bottom.
Sadness makes you feel cold-blooded.

Aliya Nsemoh (8)
Leopold Primary School, Willesden

My Senses Poem

Love tastes like red juicy apples ripening in the yellow sun.
Joy smells like hot pancakes about to go on your plate.
Fun looks like friends playing in the sun.
Happiness sounds like Christmas time!
Silence is like a creepy spider.

Joshua Bellot-Ryan (8)
Leopold Primary School, Willesden

Happiness

Love is as sweet as candyfloss
Joy is like tears coming down your face
Silence is like a hard-working pen
Fun is like tasty pasta in your mouth
Happiness feels like a fresh born child
Sadness is like blood not flowing in your body.

Dylan Mitchell (9)
Leopold Primary School, Willesden

Love Reminds

Love is like a pink rose which is perfect in an enchanted forest.
Love smells like a massive jar of perfume.
Love is like peace in a green long park.

Love reminds me of yellow sunflowers
when my friends give me a bunch of them.
Love reminds me of a massive pink heart
which will never break in half.

Timi Akinola (8)
Leopold Primary School, Willesden

Multi Feelings

Fun is like a tasty bun
Fun is like the big round sun
Joy is like a juicy apple
Happiness is like a sandy beach
Sadness is like a big bad storm.

Masood Ali Khalid (9)
Leopold Primary School, Willesden

Susan's Poem

Joy is like you just touched a star
Silence is like a baby sleeping
Fun is like playing hide-and-seek
Love is like a red heart
Happiness is like a newborn baby
Sadness is like the whole world ends.

Susan Currie (9)
Leopold Primary School, Willesden

My Senses Poem

Love reminds me of a red rose.
Joy reminds me of a black piano.
Silence reminds me of a black room.
Fun reminds me of my friends.
Happiness reminds me of my mum on a boat ride.
Sadness reminds me of when my father died.

Makere Mimi Powell (8)
Leopold Primary School, Willesden

Silence Colours

Silence is pink and tastes like peace.
Silence is blue and smells like flowers.
Silence is red and sounds like nothing.
Silence is purple and feels like air.
Silence is grey and looks like pink petals.
Silence is brown and makes me feel glad.

Jade Meredith (9)
Leopold Primary School, Willesden

Love

Love is as red as a rose burning in the sun
Joy really smells like pasta on your plate
Silence is like a paused game on TV
Fun is like a crowd of children playing a game
Happiness is like when it is Christmas
Sadness is like tears falling from your eyes.

Makai Payne (8)
Leopold Primary School, Willesden

My Poetry

Joy smells like a rose growing
Love smells like candyfloss
Silence smells like people sleeping
Fun smells like people playing
Happiness smells like flowers growing
Sadness smells like people crying.

Sean Guevarra (8)
Leopold Primary School, Willesden

Rapping Is The Best

R is for rhythm
A is for attention
P is for practise
P is for performing
I is for intelligent
N is for nets
G is for great

I is for important
S is for smile

T is for tough
H is for heavy
E is for Emile

B is for best
E is for extreme
S is for strong
T is for Tyson.

Emile Jesi (9)
Leopold Primary School, Willesden

My Summer Holiday

I will bring my colourful bikini,
I will bring my lovely and soft shampoo,
I will bring delicious cold and iced water,
I will bring my shiny blue glittery dress.

I will bring my PSP,
I will bring my DS,
I will bring my interesting books,
I will bring my Mac,
I will bring my fun games.

I will definitely bring my gorgeous phone.

Ines Santos (9)
Leopold Primary School, Willesden

Summer

When it's summer
I take lots of things
Which are sunglasses,
Make-up and silvery golden earrings.
But when I think I want a friend
I should ask my mum
Oh I almost forgot
My mum is in my tum.

When it's summer
I go up and down
Mostly where I go to
Is a shop in town
I shop and shop
Until my bags are full
I always learn French
A jumper is called la pull.

Jade Gregory (9)
Leopold Primary School, Willesden

Dat's De Truth Ruth!

I'm so fast I'm back before I'm gone.
Dat's de truth Ruth!
I'm so hot, you can fry an egg on my hand.
Dat's de truth Ruth!
I'm so strong, I could make China and Japan one.
Dat's de truth Ruth!

I'm so tall I could see space from my bedroom.
Dat's de truth Ruth!
I'm so smart, the world's greatest scientist was replaced by me.
Dat's de truth Ruth!
I'm so rich that I could afford Jupiter and Saturn alone.
Dat's de truth Ruth!

Opeyemi Orimoloye (9)
Leopold Primary School, Willesden

Colours Of The World

Red is the colour of blood
Blue is the colour of the sky
Purple is the colour of my uniform
Yellow is the colour of the sun
Green is the colour of the grass
Pink is the colour of rosy cheeks
Orange is the colour of my ink
Black is the colour of my hair
Brown is the colour of tree trunks.

Tyriesha Clarke (9)
Leopold Primary School, Willesden

Friendship

F is for faithful
R is for reply
I is for intelligent
E is for think of everybody
N is for be nearby for your friend
D is for decide on friendship
S is for superstar
H is for help your friend
I is for interest in your friend
P is for a perfect friend.

Lydia Jagroo (9)
Leopold Primary School, Willesden

Fantastic

F is for faithfulness you should have in everyone
A is for achievements you have
N is for nice and neat people are
T is for trustworthy everyone should be
A is for amazing and alert you should be
S is for super cool you are
T is for thoughtful everyone is
I is for intelligent you are
C is for caring people are towards you.

Lucie Lognon (9)
Leopold Primary School, Willesden

Leopold School

L is for learning
E is for excellent
O is for overgood
P is for power
O is for outside
L is for living
D is for doing what is expected.

S is for snack
C is for cake
H is for hush
O is for overdrive
O is for overcome
L is for love.

Adetomiwa Adenaike (9)
Leopold Primary School, Willesden

The Colour Poem

Pink, purple, black and grey,
Yellow, green and blue,
These are the colours that I will happily give to you.

Brown and white,
Red, violet and orange,
These are the colours that I will happily put in my porridge.

My favourite colours are here today,
I would happily make them into hay.

Rose Ellington (9)
Leopold Primary School, Willesden

Half Term Is Fun!

Happiness is all around us,
Amazing sights we will see,
Laughter and giggles at all my jokes,
Funny films we will buy.

Talking lots because you are so excited,
Enjoy your half term while it lasts,
Remember always your maths and subjects,
Mind you, don't forget your homework.

Is your mum busy at work?
So why not enjoy your holiday?

Fun with you and me.

Ella Mae Stodart (9)
Leopold Primary School, Willesden

Emotions

Love is white: like a peaceful dove flying in the sky.
Love is white: like people singing beautifully in the white snow.
Fun is yellow: like the blazing hot yellow sun watching the
                                            children play.
Fun is yellow: like the yellow ice cream that the children
                                            are eating.
Happiness is red: like a beautiful red rose giving out happiness.
Happiness is red: like children making others feel good inside
                                            their red heart.
Sadness is black: like a clash of thunder.
Sadness is black: like a kid's heart being ripped apart.
Joy is orange: like a kid having fun in the orange sun.
Joy is orange: like a bright orange sun on a beautiful hot day.

Rachel Carter (8)
St Agnes' RC Primary School, Cricklewood

Emotions And Feelings

Love is white like a dove floating in the air.
Love is pink like a rose given to you by somebody.
Pain is red like the blood dripping down from your cut.
Pain is peach like the peach plaster given to you by your nurse.
Joy is yellow like the sun shining upon you when you are playing with your friend.
Joy is green like the green grass you step on when you play.
Surprises are orange like the wrapping paper of your surprising birthday present.
Surprises are red like the surprise your mum gives you can be shocking and painful.
Courage is yellow like the light and warmth given to you by your friend.
Courage is purple like the colour purple on your friend's jumper.
Terror is black like the darkness around you.
Terror is red like the pain in your heart.
Wonder is grey like the loneliness and confusion in your heart.
Wonder is white like the thoughts going on in your brain.

Vicky Tsouki (9)
St Agnes' RC Primary School, Cricklewood

Untitled

Love is like a red rose smelling nice.
Love is like the summer blue breeze.

Fun is like children playing in an orange bouncy castle.
Fun is like playing in clean puddles.

Happiness is like a woman married in a white dress.
Happiness is like having red strawberries.

Sadness is like walking in a black cave.
Sadness is like falling white snow.

Joy is like having delicious candyfloss.
Joy is like swimming in the blue sea in summer.

Stanley Kasombo (8)
St Agnes' RC Primary School, Cricklewood

Feelings Poem

Love is white like a dove flying in the sky.
Love is red like a heart full of joy and happiness.
Fun is silver because you enjoy it.
Fun is orange like a bird's beak singing.
Happiness is pink like your lips laughing.
Happiness is yellow like a sunflower turning towards you.
Sadness is light blue like your tears coming down your face.
Sadness is green like the grass you look down at.
Joy is golden like sunlight shining upon you.
Joy is white like angels around you.

Stephanie Orleans (8)
St Agnes' RC Primary School, Cricklewood

Colourful Feelings

Love is red like a rose that's forever in bloom.
Love is white like a dove that flies high in the sky.
Fun is pink like a smile on a face.
Fun is turquoise like the flowing sea.
Happiness is silver like the stars in the sky.
Happiness is gold like the smiling sun.
Sadness is black like the night-time sky.
Sadness is blue like the tears in our eyes.
Joy is lavender like springtime flowers.
Joy is multicoloured like the world that we hold in our hearts.

Catarina Alves (8)
St Agnes' RC Primary School, Cricklewood

Emotions Poem

Love is white like angels singing in Heaven.
Love is silver like a crystal engagement ring.

Pain is red like a cut dripping with blood.
Pain is black like a bruise on your leg.

Joy is yellow like the shimmering sun.
Joy is blue like people swimming in a pool.

Surprise is indigo like a night sky shimmering with stars.
Surprise is violet like a jewel in the sand.

Courage is hazel when you are brave.
Courage is green to show you are not afraid.

Terror is brown like a tree trunk about to fall on you.
Terror is green like autumn about to come.

Wonder is white like snowflakes on your eyelashes.
Wonder is silver like a diamond in the sky.

Grace Marquez-Gately (8)
St Agnes' RC Primary School, Cricklewood

Joy

Joy is beautiful like a rainbow on a rainy day,
Joy makes me laugh,
Joy is a baby pink colour,
Joy smells like sweet daisies,
Joy feels warm and cosy,
Joy makes me happy,
Joy is like a painting,
Joy tastes tasty like a cake that's freshly baked,
Joy reminds me of when my baby brother was born.

Sinead Gallagher (9)
St Agnes' RC Primary School, Cricklewood

Love

Love is comfy like a fluffy pillow,
Love is like your heart caring for you inside,
Love is pink, red and white,
Love tastes like a new beginning.
Love is as red as blood,
Love is a delight in your body,
It smells like a rose in a summer garden,
Love means purity and happiness,
Love is a tickle.
Love is the sunset on Valentine's Day,
Love can be your hand to your heart,
It spreads around the whole wide world,
Love is as warm as the sun,
Everyone needs love!

Tiffany Eulalio (9)
St Agnes' RC Primary School, Cricklewood

Joy

Joy is like a fresh grape.
Joy is like Batman's cape.

Joy is like a light purple cloth.
Joy is like a flying moth.

Joy is like the bright sun.
Joy is like a blueberry bun.

Joy makes me think of a shiny red apple.
Joy makes me think of a baby's rattle.

Joy is happiness.
Joy is laughter.

Reece John Lyons (10)
St Agnes' RC Primary School, Cricklewood

Love

Love feels like soft ice cream
That will land in my stomach.
It's as nice as a cherry cake
In your mouth with a cherry on the top.

Red and white colours nice as
A cloud that is light.
It is my parents
Sitting together on the sofa
And my dad is red and my mum is white.

Love is like happiness
It brings joy and it exits loneliness.
It is like somebody crossing
Out the world's sadness and loneliness.

Love smells like beautiful pink roses.
The smell of it is so beautiful
Like a chocolate cake.
It is my mum cooking a cake.

Wiktoria Bednarek (10)
St Agnes' RC Primary School, Cricklewood

Anger

Anger is like falling into a red volcano.
It tastes like a poisonous red apple and rotten cheese.
It smells like flames of fire.
It looks like a villain murdering the superhero.
It sounds like a devil calling us.
It feels like a person has stabbed you in the tummy.

Aaron Boymbo (11)
St Agnes' RC Primary School, Cricklewood

Friendship/Fear

Friendship is yellow and bright
Like a dash of the rising sunlight
It is like a hundred smiles smiling your way
In every moment of the day
It feels simple and calm, fizzy and sweet
Tastes like a fizzy pineapple too sour to eat
Friendship is like a roller coaster never to end.

Fear is cold
And bold
It reminds me of a lightless night alone
It feels like the world is empty
And a little beat in your heart is thirsty
Fear is as shy as a snail
Who looks pale
Fear is like a test you're afraid of.

Natalia Kowalczyk (11)
St Agnes' RC Primary School, Cricklewood

Happy

It tastes like Rice Krispies popping in your mouth.
It smells like a lollipop.
It looks like the sun coming over the horizon.
It sounds like R 'n' B hip hop.
It feels like jumping into a swimming pool.

Callum Street (10)
St Agnes' RC Primary School, Cricklewood

Fear

Fear is the colour black
Like Hurricane Katrina in the south.
Fear tastes bitter and sour
Like a mixture of cold oatmeal flour.
Fear smells dingy and foul
Like a seaman's cabin two hundreds years ago.
Fear looks ghastly, grotesque
Like the bogeyman and his lair.
It sounds screechy and blood-curdling
Like a person in terror and captivity of murder.
What do you think about fear?

Chukwuemeka Ogakwu (10)
St Agnes' RC Primary School, Cricklewood

Hate

Hate is like black stormy clouds.
When you hate someone you feel like your head could explode!
Hate smells sweaty and nasty.
It looks like shouting at someone who is your enemy.
It feels like burning fire.
But it sounds like jumping out of anger in a deep dark tunnel.

Paulina Seegar (10)
St Agnes' RC Primary School, Cricklewood

A Haunted Town

Fear is a dark, dark cloud around me just ready to strike thunder.
I feel so red.
Fear tastes like something is just about to strike from far or near.
It smells like burning fire.
From here the moon shines bright from this sight
And the sound of yelling people.
I'm getting more and more scared of just one step forth.

Reece Lareo (10)
St Agnes' RC Primary School, Cricklewood

Love Everyone

Love tastes like a big, warm pink marshmallow.
Love smells like a rose that has just blossomed.
Love looks like someone just about to get married.
Love sounds as beautiful as an orchestra playing a quiet tune.
Love feels like a big red velvet heart.
Love is red and pink.
Love has passion and beauty.
Love should be cherished and treasured.
Love is a relationship and friendship with someone.
You should admire and give devotion to everyone you love.

Hannah Sullivan (10)
St Agnes' RC Primary School, Cricklewood

Happiness

Happiness is like the colour of yellow like a banana.
Happiness tastes like a sweet cherry pie.
Happiness smells like roasted chicken for dinner.
Happiness looks like children bursting with laughter.
Happiness sounds like joy.
Happiness feels like home.

Lance Castro (10)
St Agnes' RC Primary School, Cricklewood

If We Didn't Have Feelings

L eft alone, all alone, might be never found again!
O h it's not enjoyable, I would not be ecstatic then.
N obody there to help, a depressing loneliness that is life, the
E nd! Frightened and afraid as if someone left a knife
L ost in a pathetic wasteland yearning, to get out!
Y ou shout for help, you plead and cry and you don't forget to shout.

L ove is like an attracting light and an overflowing emotion!
O nly love can make a person feel differently.
V ery happy feels like you were swimming.
E very day of your life you love, no matter what!

Leilah Jade Bartley (9)
St Agnes' RC Primary School, Cricklewood

Love Spreads Around Me

Love feels like someone's hugging you.
Love smells like fresh lavender.
Love is coloured bright red like a robin's chest.
Love tastes like marshmallows so soft and comfortable to eat with.
Love looks like lovebirds in the lovely rough bushy tree.
Love sounds like Alexandra Burke singing for Her Majesty the Queen.
Love feels like lovely soft toy poodles
Made from chubby, soft feathers.
Love is a picture of romance.
Love takes part at a ball where people will dance with each other.
Love is like joy but much better than joy.
You can also make love with a bit of a mixture of joy,
Five spoons of care and forgiveness
And finally two more of laughter,
That is why love spreads around me.

Angeline Castro (9)
St Agnes' RC Primary School, Cricklewood

Anger

Anger is dark, dark red.
Anger tastes like a red pepper.
Anger smells of burnt pizza.
Anger looks like steam.
Anger sounds like rock music.
Anger feels like a hot kettle.
Anger is a horrible emotion.
Anger gets annoying for me.
Anger helps nobody.

Angelina Sentamu (8)
St Agnes' RC Primary School, Cricklewood

Irritation

Irritation is red.
It tastes like chilli con carne.
It smells like a petrol station
And it sounds like a dragon calling me.
It feels like a stinging nettle against my skin.

Leon Lyons (8)
St Agnes' RC Primary School, Cricklewood

Joyful!

Joy is bright pink.
It tastes like delicious pizza with all your favourite toppings.
Joy smells like a springtime flower that has bloomed
And looks like sparkles of joy in people's eyes.
Joy sounds like happiness and laughter.
Joy feels like tingling of happiness deep down inside.

Andrea Pamo Simples (8)
St Agnes' RC Primary School, Cricklewood

Anger

Anger is red.
It tastes like red chilli peppers and onions.
It smells like an old man's house.
It looks like a burning forest.
It burns your hand until your hand is all red.
Your face is so, so red
And it will burn your head off.

Lee Smith (8)
St Agnes' RC Primary School, Cricklewood

Angry

Angry is the colour red
And it tastes like hot chilli burning in my mouth.
Angry smells like burning pizza going inside my nose.
Angry looks like fierce red eyes.
Angry sounds like an enormous red flame.
Angry feels like hot red chilli going in my mouth.

Adrian Paul Lat (8)
St Agnes' RC Primary School, Cricklewood

Joy

Joy is yellow.
It looks like the bright yellow sun.
It smells like sweet bananas.
Joy tastes like sugary lemons.
Joy feels tremendously happy.
Joy makes me feel ecstatic
Like a tiger catching its prey.

Jamie Holgate (8)
St Agnes' RC Primary School, Cricklewood

A Poem About Anger And Evilness

Anger makes me feel like I live in a bin.
Anger tastes like a 100-year-old cheese!
Anger is as black as an apocalypse.
I feel anger when my big brother annoys me.
Anger tastes worse than a rotten rat.
Anger feels worse than having extra homework.
Evilness feels like frozen gold.
Evilness tastes like raw meat.
Evilness is as dark as night.
I feel evilness when people steal.

Stanley White (9)
St Agnes' RC Primary School, Cricklewood

Emotion Poem

Fear
Fear feels like someone is punching you in the stomach.
Fear smells like a burnt cold Irish stew.
Fear is a shade of pink getting destroyed by a shade of brown.
Fear tastes like cold gravy.

Loneliness
Loneliness makes you feel a cold breeze
Putting goosebumps on your arm.
Loneliness smells like precious chicken getting killed for food.
Loneliness is the colour green because green is unspecial.
Loneliness tastes like you haven't brushed your teeth in two weeks.

Freya Morrison (9)
St Agnes' RC Primary School, Cricklewood

Guess Who?

Slow walker
Big feet
Eat grass
Doesn't like munching
Hard shell
Strong
Likes insects
Strong feet.

Xavier Fernando (7)
St Agnes' RC Primary School, Cricklewood

Guess Who?

Sneaks up
Eats people
Loves meat
Fantastic finder
Fast runner
Massive eater
Crawler finder
Lives in the jungle.

Who am I?

David Oduro Kwarteng (7)
St Agnes' RC Primary School, Cricklewood

Guess Who?

Silent sneaker,
Quiet peeker,
Wild running,
Small and quiet,
Cheese eater,
Hole hider.

What am I?

Hollie Young (8)
St Agnes' RC Primary School, Cricklewood

Guess Who?

Hairy, scary
Big and fast
It's dangerous
Meat eater
People catcher
It's wild
Fierce roar
Powerful pouncer.

What am I?

Jack O'Sullivan (7)
St Agnes' RC Primary School, Cricklewood

Guess Who?

Waddle walker
Good swimmer
Funny fiddler
Black animal
White belly
Deep swimmer
Ice breaker
Fast skater.

Guess what?

Papa Opoku-Adjei (8)
St Agnes' RC Primary School, Cricklewood

How People Feel In Different Ways

I feel that love is a precious thing to have.
Freedom smells like perfume with lavender.
Sadness smells like a dirty, disgusting place
Which is terrifying to have.
Loneliness is as dark black as the dark damp rain with silly thunder.
Joy tastes like vanilla creamy yoghurt.
Fear is terrifying like a two-headed monster.
Gladness is as pure as the golden sea with pure golden lemonade.
Luck smells of a golden spray.
Danger smells of the Devil's eyes.
We all know that we have happy, sad or anything that has feelings
So stick to it, the feelings.

Nana Kwadjo Kwao-Amoako (9)
St Agnes' RC Primary School, Cricklewood

Freedom And Friendship

Freedom
Freedom feels like a hot summer's day.
The colour is hot red and it is like the hot blazing sun.
It's like fresh hot chocolate.
It will taste like a nice hot day.

Friendship
Friendship is a sign of love and forgiveness.
Friendship is like a place that is red.
It smells like a man and woman getting married.
It will taste like a person playing football.

Rhys Alves (9)
St Agnes' RC Primary School, Cricklewood

Guess Who?

Fish seizer,
Ice lander,
Egg huddler,
Brilliant swimmer,
Slow walker,
Black and white,
Smooth and lovely,
Little jumper,
Friendly friend,
Cute cuddler,
Guess who?

Shaheryar Nadeem (7)
St Agnes' RC Primary School, Cricklewood

Guess Who?

Ice lander
Fish eater
Black, white, yellow
Very small
Food snatcher
Egg cuddler
Moves ice
Winter lover
Loves water.

Mallaidh Duffy (7)
St Agnes' RC Primary School, Cricklewood

Guess Who?

Big thief
Eats acorns
Runs fast
It's small
Climbs trees
Big tail
Small climber.

Anthony Badr (7)
St Agnes' RC Primary School, Cricklewood

Guess Who?

Good climber.
Furry, friendly.
Leaf eater.
Nice, cuddly.
Funny, fluffy.
Small body.
Good hider.
Comes from Australia.

Ziemowit Jozefowski (7)
St Agnes' RC Primary School, Cricklewood

Britain Was Victorious

They think they can beat us,
but those smug Germans don't stand a chance.
I am confident that my brave little boys
will grind them into dust.

My winged hawks were unleashed onto the intruder - infested skies.
Slow, robotic tanks conquered the streets
with cannons pointed in every direction
threatening to kill all that was in their path.

Everything was set and ready to go then *poof!*
A bomb had plunged from the heavens onto my fragile little city
demolishing everything in sight.
The town had been obliterated and now was in tatters
but the Queen Mum and I were compelled to go on for the victory
of Britain.

Ayana Moore (11)
St James' CE Junior School, Forest Gate

Royal Air Force

There I was,
Flying into Germany at lightning speed,
We flew over German tanks,
Dropping bombs on them,
They didn't stand a chance.

The bombs filled the air with acrid smoke,
The tanks demolished,
They retreated,
To a lifeless field strewn with bodies.

We headed back to Britain,
To announce our victory for today,
But for tomorrow, only God knows!

Mitchel Chappell (11)
St James' CE Junior School, Forest Gate

RAF

There I flew,
At lightning speed,
Swooping down from the heavens,
Dropping bombs,
Destroying fields,
Creating destruction,
The sky was filled,
With intense smoke.

Metal encased killers,
Trying to kill us.
There was utter silence,
The gunfire came flying by,
The silence was broken.
It was a bloody sight,
Germans defeated,
Britain victorious.

Sami Sidhom (10)
St James' CE Junior School, Forest Gate

Heroes And Heroines · Anne Frank

The pale wall gazed at me
Telling me to go and be free

The frosty window frowned at me
Spanking me as it was unhappy

The long silk curtains hugged me
As I cried for death

The old-fashioned wooden floors
Told me to get a life

One day everything was gone
All I had left was my soul.

Ameera Kidiya (10)
St James' CE Junior School, Forest Gate

Spitfires

Big red metal machines race
Through the air
Shooting thunderous bullets
That rip through the skies.

Bellowing bombs distort the area
Bringing all but comfort
Houses destroyed, burnt to the ground.

Acrid fumes fill the air
Babies crying
Everyone choking
Then we all heard

Britain's victories.

Kyran Weekes (10)
St James' CE Junior School, Forest Gate

Anne Frank

I was sitting uncomfortably,
The wall was staring at me,
Glancing weirdly.

I could hear all the voices outside,
I felt ill,
Staying locked up under house arrest,
No air was being felt,
I could not survive,
I tried getting used to being trapped.

Anika Islam (10)
St James' CE Junior School, Forest Gate

Royal Air Force

There I flew,
At lightning speed.
My life flashing past me
Like a big eagle swooping down
From the heavens.

Whizzing in the sky,
A deadly creature attacks.
Its eyes like a furious tiger
Waiting to approach its prey.

Ripping through the sky,
My blades attacked its enemy
Breaking the other planes to bits,
I flew past as quick as lightning.

Katherine Strasser-Williams (10)
St James' CE Junior School, Forest Gate

Spitfires

The smell of the land was horrible
Everyone was glum
The skies were full of doom
We raced through the skies
Like lightning speed
I could hear gunshots like they were over my shoulder.

The sky had a thick black
Layer of smoke over it
Like a panther's coat.
I watched the bombs drop
One by one
Destroying everything in their paths.

A nightmare was unleashed
From its box
It flew into the sky.

Kennedee Chappell (11)
St James' CE Junior School, Forest Gate

Royal Air Force

There I flew,
At lightning speed,
My life flashing before me,
Like a majestic eagle swooping
Down from the heavens.

Ripping through the sky,
A deadly metal monster,
Attacks,
Its eyes like a furious lion,
Ready to attack its prey.

Theodore Nelson (10)
St James' CE Junior School, Forest Gate

Stuck In The Attic

Here I am in this darkened room.
Not alone but with my family.
I grew tired of walking on the wooden floor again and again.
Every time I lit a candle,
I can hear a voice say,
'Don't stop now, carry on!'

The wooden hard wall kept on slowly staring at me,
It was disturbing,
I wanted to open the door but it said,
'Please Anne Frank, don't open me!'

Nazifa Shahjahan (10)
St James' CE Junior School, Forest Gate

Churchill

The admirable prime minister,
Always at the right place;
Giving orders at the right time.

He was a roaring lion,
Ready to sense something
When it goes wrong.

When Hitler put out our light,
Churchill and the Queen Mother;
Were always at our side.

Churchill was a man of goodwill,
A man of no seasons;
He was like a helping hand to the nation.

Britain will always remember him
As a man of life-saving potential.

Sean Diasonoma (10)
St James' CE Junior School, Forest Gate

The Beach

I want to go to the beach as far as we can reach
I want to teach fluffy white sheep
I always use speech
So that I can teach
Please can we go to the beach
As far as we can reach.

Jawairya Mahboob (7)
St James' CE Junior School, Forest Gate

Surprise

Surprise is colourful, different colours: blue, red, green and yellow.
It smells like a nice smell and it smells like someone's there for you.
It tastes like a nice day and very cool fresh air, just coming
                                                                         in and out.
It looks like a gift from God/Allah and a friend, it also looks beautiful.
It sounds very cool and it sounds windy, like the trees rattling.
It feels so comfortable with my family and relatives saying, '*Surprise.*'

Sonia Khanum (10)
St Michael's CE Primary School, Camden

Wonder?

Wonder feels like a big question mark in my heart.
Wonder reminds me of when I met Miss Mehrnoosh.
Wonder sounds like an angel from Heaven singing 'Ah . . .'
Wonder smells like a bottle of Chanel perfume.
Wonder tastes like a bundle of joy.
Wonder looks like peace and calmness within the soul of a person.

Sophie Grace Cooper (9)
St Michael's CE Primary School, Camden

Fun

Fun reminds me of what I do
With the best teacher in the world.

Fun looks like happiness
That I get with my teacher.

Fun is colourful because
It feels like I'm riding on a rainbow.

Fun feels like playing
With my friend.

Run tastes like
Fresh food.

Fun sounds like
Birds singing.

Kabirul Hassan (9)
St Michael's CE Primary School, Camden

Untitled

Love is the colour red because roses are red.
Love looks like someone being kind.
Love smells of beautiful flowers.
Love sounds peaceful.
Love feels like you're in Heaven.
Love looks like a bunch of red roses.
Love tastes like chocolate melting in the lovely sun.

Rumana Begum (9)
St Michael's CE Primary School, Camden

Pain

Pain looks like someone getting hit and killed.
Pain is a black colour.
Pain feels like racism and hatred.
Pain reminds me of the slavery times when people suffered.
Pain tastes like blood from a sick child.
Pain sounds like injured kids shouting for help.
Pain smells of dead people.

Kalyss N'tula Leonardo (9)
St Michael's CE Primary School, Camden

Anger

Anger is red, yellow and orange fire flames.
Anger feels like burning all around you in your body
and on your face.
Anger is a negative feeling waiting to burst out.
Anger smells like trouble rustling up waiting there for you.
Anger sounds loud of your shouting voice.
Anger tastes like spicy, hot peppers and chillies
burning your tongue like acid.
Anger reminds me of fights I've seen.
Anger is a feeling of which I'm not very keen.

Miyah Susanna Flavius-Lawrence (9)
St Michael's CE Primary School, Camden

Love Is In Your Heart

It smells like love never goes away
It feels like love makes blood red like a heart
Love looks like something that comes out of your butt
Love sounds like you are married
It tastes like you're eating your heart
It reminds me of going out and spreading my love.

Mohomed Adul Wasim (9)
St Michael's CE Primary School, Camden

Surprise!

Surprise reminds me of when I went to Pizza Hut
And my family came.
Surprise looks like the water in your eyes bursting to come out
And fill the room with happiness.
Surprise sounds like the people shouting out the word we all know.
Surprise.
Surprise smells of sweet food
Which released a surprisingly nice smell.
Surprise tastes like the happiness from you which you love.
Surprise feels like everyone wants to be there for you
And cares about your feelings.
Surprise is the colours everyone's wearing.

Darmonelle Johnson (9)
St Michael's CE Primary School, Camden

Happiness

Happiness is playing with my brother in the park.
Happiness looks like someone playing.
Happiness sounds like joy floating in the air.
Happiness is yellow, as happy as ever.
Happiness tastes good like walking on air.
Happiness feels like dancing in a castle.
Happiness smells like fresh air when you go out of your house.

Mark Omoboriowo (9)
St Michael's CE Primary School, Camden

Love

It reminds me of playing football because it's fun.
Love is red because it is colourful,
Because the heart is red and it represents love.
Love tastes like when someone's saying, 'I love you.'
Love smells of joy and playing with your brother or sister.
Love feels like someone is having fun and joy with you.
Love looks like someone is having fun and joy.
Love sounds like birds singing and people laughing.

Zak Shah (9)
St Michael's CE Primary School, Camden

Happiness

Happiness tastes like my favourite food.
Happiness smells of roses.
Happiness feels like your friend.
Happiness is the colour of yellow for fun.
Happiness reminds me of break.
Happiness looks like friends.
Happiness sounds like friends.

Abdo Khadir (10)
St Michael's CE Primary School, Camden

Wonder

Wonder smells like the world gets better.
When I hear wonder it makes me feel happy.
Wonder feels like you are going to have a fabulous day.
The colour of wonder is a bunch of lovely roses.
Wonder reminds me of dark chocolate with tea.
Wonder tastes like honey and then bees get jealous.
Wonder looks like a river
And the waves make the water look beautiful.

Hamida Aktar (9)
St Michael's CE Primary School, Camden

Wonder

Wonder is light blue like the waves of an ocean.
Wonder smells like milk chocolate melting in the sun.
Wonder looks like the yellow sun shining in the dark blue sky.
Wonder feels like swimming around in the turquoise sea.
Wonder reminds me of all the fun I have with my friends.
Wonder tastes like lasagne freshly made.
Wonder sounds like bees buzzing around in the summer skies.

Masuma Chowdhury (9)
St Michael's CE Primary School, Camden

Anger

Anger is disrespect like breaking someone's heart,
Anger is like being reminded of getting in a fight,
Anger tastes bitter like eating a big wasp,
Anger is the colour of darkness like scary black monsters,
Anger is sadness like being shouted at,
Anger smells revolting like horrible compost,
Anger looks fierce like being attacked by a ferocious lion.

Anger hurts.

Munadia Hussain (9)
St Michael's CE Primary School, Camden

Pain!

Pain smells of hurt like someone has poisoned you.
Pain reminds you of sadness like it is going to make you feel lonely and no one will like you.
Pain is the colour of black because pain makes you terrified.
Pain looks like no one want to see it.
Pain sounds like a person screaming in your ear
because that's how bad it is.
Pain tastes like old lumps of bread that give you a bad tummy ache.
Pain feels it is destroying your soul.

Ismail Uddin (10)
St Michael's CE Primary School, Camden

Silence!

Silence smells of fresh air.
I think silence is white because
Of the expression you can feel.
It's like tasting a handful of your favourite food.
I think silence looks like flowers,
Sunset and the waves at the seaside.
It reminds me of all the good times
I have had in a different country.
It feels like a great, special, calm moment.

Vesa Sponca (9)
St Michael's CE Primary School, Camden

Fun!

Fun is the favourite feeling anyone can get.
Fun is light blue like the sky shining bright.
Fun reminds me of when it was the best day of my life.
Fun smells like the fresh air outside in the wind blowing lightly.
Fun looks like swimming in the pool,
Splashing and throwing balls around.
Fun sounds like children playing in the park
And getting really excited.

Fjolla Aliu (10)
St Michael's CE Primary School, Camden

Love

Love is love,
Love is peace,
Love always sounds like people hugging and smiling,
Love always looks like families playing and hugging
And love reminds me of mums and dads,
Love smells like eating something nice,
Now that's how love fills me.

Love is love,
Love is peace,
Love can live in all your dreams,
Love makes the world entwined,
All you do is
Love it,
Feel it
And make it.
Love.

Isabelle Rolston (10)
St Michael's CE Primary School, Camden

Love

Love tastes wonderful because it is happiness
It smells like happiness because love is happiness
It reminds you that love is someone you love
It feels like you are in love and it's happiness
Love sounds like a special kiss
The colour of love can be any colour you imagine.

Mirza Parvez (10)
St Michael's CE Primary School, Camden

Courage

Courage reminds me of something I've done kind to my mum.
Courage is the colour of yellow like self-control.
Courage smells like flowers.
It feels like something you have done good.
It tastes like breakfast in the morning.
Sounds like music.

Dary N'tula Leonardo (9)
St Michael's CE Primary School, Camden

Young Writers Information

We hope you have enjoyed reading this book - and that you will continue to enjoy it in the coming years.

If you like reading and writing poetry drop us a line, or give us a call, and we'll send you a free information pack.

Alternatively if you would like to order further copies of this book or any of our other titles, then please give us a call or log onto our website at www.youngwriters.co.uk.

Young Writers Information
Remus House
Coltsfoot Drive
Peterborough
PE2 9JX
(01733) 890066